UNDATED WEEKLY & MONTHLY VIEW
GOAL SETTING PLANNER

If you find this, please be kind and contact me..

Name ....
Phone ....
Email ....
Social ....

Your reward ....

Awareness & Self Discovery

What brings me joy in life? What am I passionate about?

What would I do if money wasn't an issue?

What are my personal core values?

What does a perfect 'day in the life' look like for me?

What does a successful life look like for me?

My Goals & Dreams

Write down your goals and dreams in all areas of your life

- Career & Business
- Health & fitness
- Finance & Net Worth
- Romance & Relationships
- MY LIFE GOALS
- Family & Friends
- Personal Development
- Fun & Hobbies
- Spiritual

My Vision Board

My 1 Year Goals

Health & Fitness		
Fun & Hobbies		
Personal Development		
Family & Friends		
Romance & Relationships		
Finance & Net Worth		
Career & Business		
Spiritual		

My 3 Month Goals

"This one step—choosing a goal and sticking to it—changes everything."

Goal 1

How I'll achieve it	Reward if achieved

Goal 2

How I'll achieve it	Reward if achieved

Goal 3

How I'll achieve it	Reward if achieved

My 3 Month Goals

"This one step—choosing a goal and sticking to it—changes everything."

Goal 1

How I'll achieve it | Reward if achieved

Goal 2

How I'll achieve it | Reward if achieved

Goal 3

How I'll achieve it | Reward if achieved

My 3 Month Goals

"This one step—choosing a goal and sticking to it—changes everything."

Goal 1

How I'll achieve it	Reward if achieved

Goal 2

How I'll achieve it	Reward if achieved

Goal 3

How I'll achieve it	Reward if achieved

My 3 Month Goals

"This one step—choosing a goal and sticking to it—changes everything."

Goal 1

How I'll achieve it

Reward if achieved

Goal 2

How I'll achieve it

Reward if achieved

Goal 3

How I'll achieve it

Reward if achieved

Month:

Monthly Planner

Monday	Tuesday	Wednesday	Thursday	Friday	Saturday	Sunday

NOTES...

My most important goals to make this month great

My most important goals to make this month great

My most important goals to make this month great

REFLECT...

3 important lessons I've learned this month?

This month's win's are…

Which life areas could improve next month?

What I'll do to make next month great:

Month: Monthly Planner

Monday	Tuesday	Wednesday	Thursday	Friday	Saturday	Sunday

NOTES...

My most important goals to make this month great

My most important goals to make this month great

My most important goals to make this month great

REFLECT

3 important lessons I've learned this month?

This month's win's are…

Which life areas could improve next month?

What I'll do to make next month great:

Month:

Monthly Planner

Monday	Tuesday	Wednesday	Thursday	Friday	Saturday	Sunday

NOTES...

My most important goals to make this month great

My most important goals to make this month great

My most important goals to make this month great

REFLECT...

3 important lessons I've learned this month?

This month's win's are…

Which life areas could improve next month?

What I'll do to make next month great:

Month:

Monthly Planner

Monday	Tuesday	Wednesday	Thursday	Friday	Saturday	Sunday

NOTES...

My most important goals to make this month great

My most important goals to make this month great

My most important goals to make this month great

REFLECT

3 important lessons I've learned this month?

This month's win's are…

Which life areas could improve next month?

What I'll do to make next month great.

Month:

Monthly Planner

Monday	Tuesday	Wednesday	Thursday	Friday	Saturday	Sunday

NOTES...

My most important goals to make this month great

My most important goals to make this month great

My most important goals to make this month great

REFLECT...

3 important lessons I've learned this month?

This month's win's are…

Which life areas could improve next month?

What I'll do to make next month great:

Month:

Monthly Planner

Monday	Tuesday	Wednesday	Thursday	Friday	Saturday	Sunday

NOTES

My most important goals to make this month great

My most important goals to make this month great

My most important goals to make this month great

REFLECT

3 important lessons I've learned this month?

This month's win's are…

Which life areas could improve next month?

What I'll do to make next month great:

Month:

Monthly Planner

Monday	Tuesday	Wednesday	Thursday	Friday	Saturday	Sunday

NOTES...

My most important goals to make this month great

My most important goals to make this month great

My most important goals to make this month great

REFLECT...

3 important lessons I've learned this month?

This month's win's are…

Which life areas could improve next month?

What I'll do to make next month great:

Month: Monthly Planner

Monday	Tuesday	Wednesday	Thursday	Friday	Saturday	Sunday

NOTES

My most important goals to make this month great

My most important goals to make this month great

My most important goals to make this month great

REFLECT

3 important lessons I've learned this month?

This month's win's are...

Which life areas could improve next month?

What I'll do to make next month great:

Month:

Monthly Planner

Monday	Tuesday	Wednesday	Thursday	Friday	Saturday	Sunday

NOTES...

My most important goals to make this month great

My most important goals to make this month great

My most important goals to make this month great

REFLECT...

3 important lessons I've learned this month?

This month's win's are…

Which life areas could improve next month?

What I'll do to make next month great:

Month:

Monthly Planner

Monday	Tuesday	Wednesday	Thursday	Friday	Saturday	Sunday

NOTES:

My most important goals to make this month great

My most important goals to make this month great

My most important goals to make this month great

REFLECT

3 important lessons I've learned this month?

This month's win's are…

Which life areas could improve next month?

What I'll do to make next month great:

Month:

Monthly Planner

Monday	Tuesday	Wednesday	Thursday	Friday	Saturday	Sunday

NOTES...

My most important goals to make this month great

My most important goals to make this month great

My most important goals to make this month great

REFLECT...

3 important lessons I've learned this month?

This month's win's are…

Which life areas could improve next month?

What I'll do to make next month great:

Month:

Monthly Planner

Monday	Tuesday	Wednesday	Thursday	Friday	Saturday	Sunday

NOTES

My most important goals to make this month great

My most important goals to make this month great

My most important goals to make this month great

REFLECT

3 important lessons I've learned this month?

This month's win's are…

Which life areas could improve next month?

What I'll do to make next month great:

Month: _____

Monthly Planner

Monday	Tuesday	Wednesday	Thursday	Friday	Saturday	Sunday

NOTES...

_____
_____
_____
_____

My most important goals to make this month great

My most important goals to make this month great

My most important goals to make this month great

REFLECT...

3 important lessons I've learned this month?

This month's win's are…

Which life areas could improve next month?

What I'll do to make next month great:

Month:

Weekly Planner

Each day, aim to write:
- *A to do list*
- *What you're grateful for that day*
- *A self care activity you'll complete*

Mon

Tue

Wed

Thu

Fri

Sat

Sun

Morning Routine:

Habit Tracker:

M T W T F S S

This weeks main goal:

Evening routine:

Reward if achieved:

Month:

Weekly Planner

Each day, aim to write:
- A to do list
- What you're grateful for that day
- A self care activity you'll complete

Mon

Tue

Wed

Thu

Fri

Sat

Sun

Morning Routine:

Habit Tracker:

M T W T F S S

Evening routine:

This weeks main goal:

Reward if achieved:

Month:

Weekly Planner

Each day, aim to write:
- A to do list
- What you're grateful for that day
- A self care activity you'll complete

Mon

Tue

Wed

Thu

Fri

Sat

Sun

Morning Routine:

Habit Tracker:

M	T	W	T	F	S	S

This weeks main goal:

Evening routine:

Reward if achieved:

Month:

Weekly Planner

Each day, aim to write:
- *A to do list*
- *What you're grateful for that day*
- *A self care activity you'll complete*

Mon

Tue

Wed

Thu

Fri

Sat

Sun

Morning Routine:

Habit Tracker:

M T W T F S S

This weeks main goal:

Evening routine:

Reward if achieved:

Month:

Weekly Planner

Each day, aim to write:
- *A to do list*
- *What you're grateful for that day*
- *A self care activity you'll complete*

Mon

Tue

Wed

Thu

Fri

Sat

Sun

Morning Routine.

Habit Tracker:

M T W T F S S

This weeks main goal:

Evening routine:

Reward if achieved:

Month: | Weekly Planner | Each day, aim to write:
- A to do list
- What you're grateful for that day
- A self care activity you'll complete

Mon

Tue

Wed

Thu

Fri

Sat

Sun

Morning Routine:

Habit Tracker:

	M	T	W	T	F	S	S

This weeks main goal:

Evening routine:

Reward if achieved:

Month:

Weekly Planner

Each day, aim to write:
- A to do list
- What you're grateful for that day
- A self care activity you'll complete

Mon

Tue

Wed

Thu

Fri

Sat

Sun

Morning Routine:

Habit Tracker:

M T W T F S S

This weeks main goal:

Evening routine:

Reward if achieved:

Month: _____   Weekly Planner

Each day, aim to write:
- A to do list
- What you're grateful for that day
- A self care activity you'll complete

Mon

Tue

Wed

Thu

Fri

Sat

Sun

Morning Routine:

Habit Tracker:

M T W T F S S

This weeks main goal:

Evening routine:

Reward if achieved:

Month:

Weekly Planner

Each day, aim to write:
- A to do list
- What you're grateful for that day
- A self care activity you'll complete

Mon

Tue

Wed

Thu

Fri

Sat

Sun

Morning Routine:

Habit Tracker:

M T W T F S S

This weeks main goal:

Evening routine:

Reward if achieved:

Month:

Weekly Planner

Each day, aim to write:
- A to do list
- What you're grateful for that day
- A self care activity you'll complete

Mon

Tue

Wed

Thu

Fri

Sat

Sun

Morning Routine:

Habit Tracker:

M T W T F S S

This weeks main goal:

Evening routine:

Reward if achieved:

Month:

Weekly Planner

Each day, aim to write:
- *A to do list*
- *What you're grateful for that day*
- *A self care activity you'll complete*

Mon

Tue

Wed

Thu

Fri

Sat

Sun

Morning Routine:

Habit Tracker:

M T W T F S S

This weeks main goal:

Evening routine:

Reward if achieved:

Month: _____

Weekly Planner

Each day, aim to write:
- A to do list
- What you're grateful for that day
- A self care activity you'll complete

Mon

Tue

Wed

Thu

Fri

Sat

Sun

Morning Routine:

Habit Tracker:

	M	T	W	T	F	S	S
	☐	☐	☐	☐	☐	☐	☐
	☐	☐	☐	☐	☐	☐	☐
	☐	☐	☐	☐	☐	☐	☐
	☐	☐	☐	☐	☐	☐	☐

This weeks main goal:

Evening routine:

Reward if achieved:

Month:

Weekly Planner

Each day, aim to write:
- A to do list
- What you're grateful for that day
- A self care activity you'll complete

Mon

Tue

Wed

Thu

Fri

Sat

Sun

Morning Routine:

Habit Tracker:

	M	T	W	T	F	S	S

This weeks main goal:

Evening routine:

Reward if achieved:

Month:

Weekly Planner

Each day, aim to write:
- A to do list
- What you're grateful for that day
- A self care activity you'll complete

Mon

Tue

Wed

Thu

Fri

Sat

Sun

Morning Routine:

Habit Tracker:

	M	T	W	T	F	S	S

This weeks main goal:

Evening routine:

Reward if achieved:

Month:

Weekly Planner

Each day, aim to write:
- A to do list
- What you're grateful for that day
- A self care activity you'll complete

Mon

Tue

Wed

Thu

Fri

Sat

Sun

Morning Routine:

Habit Tracker:

M T W T F S S

This weeks main goal:

Evening routine:

Reward if achieved:

Month:

Weekly Planner

Each day, aim to write:
- A to do list
- What you're grateful for that day
- A self care activity you'll complete

Mon

Tue

Wed

Thu

Fri

Sat

Sun

Morning Routine:

Habit Tracker:

M T W T F S S

This weeks main goal:

Evening routine:

Reward if achieved:

Month:

Weekly Planner

Each day, aim to write:
- A to do list
- What you're grateful for that day
- A self care activity you'll complete

Mon

Tue

Wed

Thu

Fri

Sat

Sun

Morning Routine:

Habit Tracker:

M T W T F S S

This weeks main goal:

Evening routine:

Reward if achieved:

Month: | Weekly Planner | Each day, aim to write:
- A to do list
- What you're grateful for that day
- A self care activity you'll complete

Mon

Tue

Wed

Thu

Fri

Sat

Sun

Morning Routine:

Habit Tracker:

	M	T	W	T	F	S	S

This weeks main goal:

Evening routine:

Reward if achieved:

Month:

Weekly Planner

Each day, aim to write:
- *A to do list*
- *What you're grateful for that day*
- *A self care activity you'll complete*

Mon

Tue

Wed

Thu

Fri

Sat

Sun

Morning Routine:

Habit Tracker:

M	T	W	T	F	S	S

This weeks main goal:

Evening routine:

Reward if achieved:

Month:

Weekly Planner

Each day, aim to write:
- *A to do list*
- *What you're grateful for that day*
- *A self care activity you'll complete*

Mon

Tue

Wed

Thu

Fri

Sat

Sun

Morning Routine:

Habit Tracker:

M	T	W	T	F	S	S

This weeks main goal:

Evening routine:

Reward if achieved:

Month:

Weekly Planner

Each day, aim to write:
- A to do list
- What you're grateful for that day
- A self care activity you'll complete

Mon

Tue

Wed

Thu

Fri

Sat

Sun

Morning Routine:

Habit Tracker:

M T W T F S S

This weeks main goal:

Evening routine:

Reward if achieved:

Month:

Weekly Planner

Each day, aim to write:
- A to do list
- What you're grateful for that day
- A self care activity you'll complete

Mon

Tue

Wed

Thu

Fri

Sat

Sun

Morning Routine:

Habit Tracker:

M T W T F S S

This weeks main goal:

Evening routine:

Reward if achieved:

Month:

Weekly Planner

Each day, aim to write:
- *A to do list*
- *What you're grateful for that day*
- *A self care activity you'll complete*

Mon

Tue

Wed

Thu

Fri

Sat

Sun

Morning Routine:

Habit Tracker:

M	T	W	T	F	S	S

This weeks main goal:

Evening routine:

Reward if achieved:

Month:

Weekly Planner

Each day, aim to write:
- *A to do list*
- *What you're grateful for that day*
- *A self care activity you'll complete*

Mon

Tue

Wed

Thu

Fri

Sat

Sun

Morning Routine:

Habit Tracker:

	M	T	W	T	F	S	S

This weeks main goal:

Evening routine:

Reward if achieved:

Month:

Weekly Planner

Each day, aim to write:
- A to do list
- What you're grateful for that day
- A self care activity you'll complete

Mon

Tue

Wed

Thu

Fri

Sat

Sun

Morning Routine:

Habit Tracker:

M T W T F S S

This weeks main goal:

Evening routine:

Reward if achieved:

Month:

Weekly Planner

Each day, aim to write:
- *A to do list*
- *What you're grateful for that day*
- *A self care activity you'll complete*

Mon

Tue

Wed

Thu

Fri

Sat

Sun

Morning Routine:

Habit Tracker:

| M | T | W | T | F | S | S |

This weeks main goal:

Evening routine:

Reward if achieved:

Month:

Weekly Planner

Each day, aim to write:
- *A to do list*
- *What you're grateful for that day*
- *A self care activity you'll complete*

Mon

Tue

Wed

Thu

Fri

Sat

Sun

Morning Routine.

Habit Tracker:

M T W T F S S

This weeks main goal:

Evening routine:

Reward if achieved:

Month:

Weekly Planner

Each day, aim to write:
- A to do list
- What you're grateful for that day
- A self care activity you'll complete

Mon

Tue

Wed

Thu

Fri

Sat

Sun

Morning Routine:

Habit Tracker:

	M	T	W	T	F	S	S

This weeks main goal:

Evening routine:

Reward if achieved:

Month:

Weekly Planner

Each day, aim to write:
- A to do list
- What you're grateful for that day
- A self care activity you'll complete

Mon

Tue

Wed

Thu

Fri

Sat

Sun

Morning Routine:

Habit Tracker:

	M	T	W	T	F	S	S

This weeks main goal:

Evening routine:

Reward if achieved:

Month:

Weekly Planner

Each day, aim to write:
- A to do list
- What you're grateful for that day
- A self care activity you'll complete

Mon

Tue

Wed

Thu

Fri

Sat

Sun

Morning Routine:

Habit Tracker:

M T W T F S S

This weeks main goal:

Evening routine:

Reward if achieved:

Month:

Weekly Planner

Each day, aim to write:
- A to do list
- What you're grateful for that day
- A self care activity you'll complete

Mon

Tue

Wed

Thu

Fri

Sat

Sun

Morning Routine:

Habit Tracker:

M T W T F S S

This weeks main goal:

Evening routine:

Reward if achieved:

Month:

Weekly Planner

Each day, aim to write:
- *A to do list*
- *What you're grateful for that day*
- *A self care activity you'll complete*

Mon

Tue

Wed

Thu

Fri

Sat

Sun

Morning Routine:

Habit Tracker:

	M	T	W	T	F	S	S

This weeks main goal:

Evening routine:

Reward if achieved:

Month:

Weekly Planner

Each day, aim to write:
- *A to do list*
- *What you're grateful for that day*
- *A self care activity you'll complete*

Mon

Tue

Wed

Thu

Fri

Sat

Sun

Morning Routine.

Habit Tracker:

M	T	W	T	F	S	S

This weeks main goal:

Evening routine:

Reward if achieved:

Month: _____

Weekly Planner

Each day, aim to write:
- A to do list
- What you're grateful for that day
- A self care activity you'll complete

Mon

Tue

Wed

Thu

Fri

Sat

Sun

Morning Routine:

Habit Tracker:

	M	T	W	T	F	S	S
	☐	☐	☐	☐	☐	☐	☐
	☐	☐	☐	☐	☐	☐	☐
	☐	☐	☐	☐	☐	☐	☐
	☐	☐	☐	☐	☐	☐	☐

This weeks main goal:

Evening routine:

Reward if achieved:

Month:

Weekly Planner

Each day, aim to write:
- A to do list
- What you're grateful for that day
- A self care activity you'll complete

Mon

Tue

Wed

Thu

Fri

Sat

Sun

Morning Routine:

Habit Tracker:

M	T	W	T	F	S	S

This weeks main goal:

Evening routine:

Reward if achieved:

Month:

Weekly Planner

Each day, aim to write:
- A to do list
- What you're grateful for that day
- A self care activity you'll complete

Mon

Tue

Wed

Thu

Fri

Sat

Sun

Morning Routine:

Habit Tracker:

M T W T F S S

This weeks main goal:

Evening routine:

Reward if achieved:

Month:	## Weekly Planner

Each day, aim to write:
- A to do list
- What you're grateful for that day
- A self care activity you'll complete

☐ **Mon**

☐ **Tue**

☐ **Wed**

☐ **Thu**

☐ **Fri**

☐ **Sat**

☐ **Sun**

Morning Routine:

Habit Tracker:

M T W T F S S

This weeks main goal:

Evening routine:

Reward if achieved:

Month:

Weekly Planner

Each day, aim to write:
- A to do list
- What you're grateful for that day
- A self care activity you'll complete

Mon

Tue

Wed

Thu

Fri

Sat

Sun

Morning Routine:

Habit Tracker:

M T W T F S S

This weeks main goal:

Evening routine:

Reward if achieved:

Month:

Weekly Planner

Each day, aim to write:
- A to do list
- What you're grateful for that day
- A self care activity you'll complete

Mon

Tue

Wed

Thu

Fri

Sat

Sun

Morning Routine:

Habit Tracker:

M T W T F S S

This weeks main goal:

Evening routine:

Reward if achieved:

Month:

Weekly Planner

Each day, aim to write:
- A to do list
- What you're grateful for that day
- A self care activity you'll complete

Mon

Tue

Wed

Thu

Fri

Sat

Sun

Morning Routine:

Habit Tracker:

M T W T F S S

This weeks main goal:

Evening routine:

Reward if achieved:

Month:

Weekly Planner

Each day, aim to write:
- *A to do list*
- *What you're grateful for that day*
- *A self care activity you'll complete*

Mon

Tue

Wed

Thu

Fri

Sat

Sun

Morning Routine:

Habit Tracker:

M T W T F S S

This weeks main goal:

Evening routine:

Reward if achieved:

Month:

Weekly Planner

Each day, aim to write:
- A to do list
- What you're grateful for that day
- A self care activity you'll complete

Mon

Tue

Wed

Thu

Fri

Sat

Sun

Morning Routine:

Habit Tracker:

M T W T F S S

This weeks main goal:

Evening routine:

Reward if achieved:

Month: Weekly Planner

Each day, aim to write:
- *A to do list*
- *What you're grateful for that day*
- *A self care activity you'll complete*

Mon

Tue

Wed

Thu

Fri

Sat   Sun

Morning Routine:	Habit Tracker:	This weeks main goal:
	M T W T F S S	
Evening routine:		Reward if achieved:

Month:

Weekly Planner

Each day, aim to write:
- A to do list
- What you're grateful for that day
- A self care activity you'll complete

Mon

Tue

Wed

Thu

Fri

Sat

Sun

Morning Routine:

Habit Tracker:

| M | T | W | T | F | S | S |

This weeks main goal:

Evening routine:

Reward if achieved:

Month:

Weekly Planner

Each day, aim to write:
- A to do list
- What you're grateful for that day
- A self care activity you'll complete

Mon

Tue

Wed

Thu

Fri

Sat

Sun

Morning Routine:

Habit Tracker:

M T W T F S S

This weeks main goal:

Evening routine:

Reward if achieved:

Month:

Weekly Planner

Each day, aim to write:
- *A to do list*
- *What you're grateful for that day*
- *A self care activity you'll complete*

Mon

Tue

Wed

Thu

Fri

Sat

Sun

Morning Routine:

Habit Tracker:

M T W T F S S

This weeks main goal:

Evening routine:

Reward if achieved:

Month:

Weekly Planner

Each day, aim to write:
- A to do list
- What you're grateful for that day
- A self care activity you'll complete

Mon

Tue

Wed

Thu

Fri

Sat

Sun

Morning Routine:

Habit Tracker:

M T W T F S S

This weeks main goal:

Evening routine:

Reward if achieved:

Month:

Weekly Planner

Each day, aim to write:
- *A to do list*
- *What you're grateful for that day*
- *A self care activity you'll complete*

Mon

Tue

Wed

Thu

Fri

Sat

Sun

Morning Routine:

Habit Tracker:

| M | T | W | T | F | S | S |

This weeks main goal:

Evening routine:

Reward if achieved:

Month:

Weekly Planner

Each day, aim to write:
- A to do list
- What you're grateful for that day
- A self care activity you'll complete

Mon

Tue

Wed

Thu

Fri

Sat

Sun

Morning Routine:

Habit Tracker:

M T W T F S S

This week's main goal:

Evening routine:

Reward if achieved:

Month:

Weekly Planner

Each day, aim to write:
- A to do list
- What you're grateful for that day
- A self care activity you'll complete

Mon

Tue

Wed

Thu

Fri

Sat

Sun

Morning Routine:

Habit Tracker:

M T W T F S S

This weeks main goal:

Evening routine:

Reward if achieved:

Month:	Weekly Planner	Each day, aim to write:

- A to do list
- What you're grateful for that day
- A self care activity you'll complete

☐ Mon

☐ Tue

☐ Wed

☐ Thu

☐ Fri

☐ Sat   ☐ Sun

Morning Routine:	Habit Tracker:	This weeks main goal:
	M T W T F S S	
Evening routine:		Reward if achieved:

Month:

Weekly Planner

Each day, aim to write:
- A to do list
- What you're grateful for that day
- A self care activity you'll complete

Mon

Tue

Wed

Thu

Fri

Sat

Sun

Morning Routine:

Habit Tracker:

	M	T	W	T	F	S	S

This weeks main goal:

Evening routine:

Reward if achieved:

Month: Example

Finance Planner

"The art is not in making money, but in keeping it."

This Month's Financial Goals

Save £500	Pay off credit card
Spend less money eating out	Make my phone bill cheaper

Total Savings

Help to buy ISA	£2000
Christmas Savings	£550
General Savings	£1300

This Months Budget

Total Income	£2000		
Outgoings		**Due**	**Paid?**
Rent	£500	1st	✓
Gas	£40	1st	✓
Electric	£45	1st	✓
Water	£40	1st	✓
TV & Broadband	£50	5th	
TV Licence	£50	1st	✓
Council Tax	£13	1st	✓
Car Finance	£200	3rd	
Petrol	£80		✓
Phone bill	£15	1st	✓
Life & Home insurance	£60	1st	✓
Food shopping	£250		✓
Christmas Savings	£50	1st	✓
Help to buy ISA	£200	1st	✓
General Savings	150	1st	✓

Disposible income £ £257

Expense Tracker

Date	Expense	Cost	Budget
2nd	Outfit for birthday	£30	£77
5th	Nandos	£15	£62
12th	New jumper	£15	£47
17th	M & D anniversary present	£30	£17

Budget for upcoming events/purchases

Date	Event	Cost
6th	My birthday	£30 outfit, £70 spends
20th	Mum & Dad Anniversary	£50
		£100

Month:

Finance Planner

"The art is not in making money, but in keeping it."

This Month's Financial Goals

Total Savings

This Months Budget

Total Income			
Outgoings		Due	Paid?

Disposible income £

Expense Tracker

Date	Expense	Cost	Budget

Budget for upcoming events/purchases

Date	Event	Cost

Month: _____   Finance Planner   *"The art is not in making money, but in keeping it."*

This Month's Financial Goals

Total Savings

This Months Budget

Total Income

Outgoings		Due	Paid?

Expense Tracker

Date	Expense	Cost	Budget

Disposible income £

Budget for upcoming events/purchases

Date	Event	Cost

Month:

Finance Planner

"The art is not in making money, but in keeping it."

This Month's Financial Goals

Total Savings

This Months Budget

Total Income			
Outgoings		Due	Paid?

Disposible income £

Expense Tracker

Date	Expense	Cost	Budget

Budget for upcoming events/purchases

Date	Event	Cost

Month:

Finance Planner

"The art is not in making money, but in keeping it."

This Month's Financial Goals

Total Savings

This Months Budget

Total Income			
Outgoings		Due	Paid?

Disposible income £

Expense Tracker

Date	Expense	Cost	Budget

Budget for upcoming events/purchases

Date	Event	Cost

Month:

Finance Planner

"The art is not in making money, but in keeping it."

This Month's Financial Goals

Total Savings

This Months Budget

Total Income

Outgoings		Due	Paid?

Disposible income £

Expense Tracker

Date	Expense	Cost	Budget

Budget for upcoming events/purchases

Date	Event	Cost

Month: **Finance Planner** *"The art is not in making money, but in keeping it."*

This Month's Financial Goals

Total Savings

This Months Budget

Total Income

Outgoings		Due	Paid?

Disposable income £

Expense Tracker

Date	Expense	Cost	Budget

Budget for upcoming events/purchases

Date	Event	Cost

Month:

Finance Planner

"The art is not in making money, but in keeping it."

This Month's Financial Goals

Total Savings

This Months Budget

Total Income			
Outgoings		Due	Paid?

Disposible income £

Expense Tracker

Date	Expense	Cost	Budget

Budget for upcoming events/purchases

Date	Event	Cost

Month: Finance Planner *"The art is not in making money, but in keeping it."*

This Month's Financial Goals

Total Savings

This Months Budget

Total Income			
Outgoings		Due	Paid?

Disposible income £

Expense Tracker

Date	Expense	Cost	Budget

Budget for upcoming events/purchases

Date	Event	Cost

Month:

Finance Planner

"The art is not in making money, but in keeping it."

This Month's Financial Goals

Total Savings

This Months Budget

Total Income			
Outgoings		Due	Paid?
Disposible income	£		

Expense Tracker

Date	Expense	Cost	Budget

Budget for upcoming events/purchases

Date	Event	Cost

Month:

Finance Planner

"The art is not in making money, but in keeping it."

This Month's Financial Goals

Total Savings

This Months Budget

Total Income

Outgoings | | Due | Paid?

Disposible income £

Expense Tracker

Date	Expense	Cost	Budget

Budget for upcoming events/purchases

Date	Event	Cost

Month:

Finance Planner

"The art is not in making money, but in keeping it."

This Month's Financial Goals

Total Savings

This Months Budget

Total Income			
Outgoings		Due	Paid?

Disposible income   £

Expense Tracker

Date	Expense	Cost	Budget

Budget for upcoming events/purchases

Date	Event	Cost

Month: _____   Finance Planner   *"The art is not in making money, but in keeping it."*

This Month's Financial Goals

Total Savings

This Months Budget

Total Income	

Outgoings		Due	Paid?

Disposible income   £

Expense Tracker

Date	Expense	Cost	Budget

Budget for upcoming events/purchases

Date	Event	Cost

NOTES

NOTES

NOTES